SHIBORI MAGIC

Transforming Fabric with Dye and Design

Table of Contents

CHAPTER ONE..**5**
  THE ART OF SHIBORI...5
    Introduction to Shibori: A Brief History.....................5
    Cultural Significance of Shibori in Japan.................6
    Shibori vs. Tie-Dye: Understanding the Differences...........8

CHAPTER TWO..**12**
  TOOLS AND MATERIALS... 12
    Fabrics: Choosing the Best Textiles for Shibori............... 12
    Essential Tools and Equipment.. 16
    Types of Dyes: Natural vs. Synthetic................................18

CHAPTER THREE..**22**
  TRADITIONAL SHIBORI TECHNIQUE................................. 22
    Kanoko (Bound) Shibori.. 22
    Miura (Looped) Shibori..24
    Kumo (Spider Web) Shibori...25
    Nui (Stitched) Shibori...27
    Arashi (Pole-Wrapped) Shibori...28
    Itajime (Clamped) Shibori..30

CHAPTER FOUR..**32**
  MODERN INTERPRETATIONS OF SHIBORI........................ 32
    Experimenting with Colors...32
    Contemporary Patterns and Designs................................ 34
    Mixing Traditional and Modern Techniques...................... 37

CHAPTER FIVE..**41**
  PREPARING THE FABRIC...41
    Washing and Pre-treating the Fabric................................41
    Folding, Pleating, and Binding Techniques...................... 43
    Achieving the Perfect Resist: Methods and Tips.............. 47

CHAPTER SIX..**50**
  DYEING TECHNIQUES...50

    Immersion Dyeing: Full Coverage Techniques................50
    Dip Dyeing: Creating Gradients and Ombres..................52
    Layering Dyes for Complex Effects................................54
    Overdyeing and Color Blending..56

CHAPTER SEVEN..59
  PATTERNS AND DESIGNS..59
    Geometric Patterns: Crisp Lines and Shapes.................59
    Organic Patterns: Freeform and Nature-Inspired Designs... 61
    Symmetry and Asymmetry in Shibori...............................64

CHAPTER EIGHT...67
  POST-DYEING CARE...67
    Rinsing and Unwrapping Your Fabric...............................67
    Setting the Dye: Fixatives and Techniques......................70
    Post-Dye Treatments: Ironing and Finishing...................72

CHAPTER NINE..75
  SHIBORI PROJECTS...75
    Home Décor: Curtains, Pillows, and Tablecloths............75
    Fashion: Scarves, Shawls, and Clothing..........................79
    Accessories: Bags, Hats, and Other Items......................82
    Large-Scale Shibori: Quilts and Wall Hangings...............84

CHAPTER TEN...87
  TROUBLESHOOTING COMMON SHIBORI PROBLEMS.....87
    Fixing Uneven Dyeing and Color Bleeding......................87
    Addressing Fabric Tearing or Overstretching.................89
    Avoiding Stains and Unwanted Marks.............................91

CHAPTER ELEVEN..94
  THE FUTURE OF SHIBORI..94
    How Shibori Continues to Evolve......................................94
    Shibori in Contemporary Fashion and Art.......................97
    Artists and Designers Inspired by Shibori........................99

CHAPTER TWELVE... 102

CONCLUSION..102
   Finding Your Unique Shibori Style..................................102
   Encouraging Creativity and Experimentation................. 104
   Final Thoughts on the Art of Shibori.............................. 106

CHAPTER ONE

THE ART OF SHIBORI

Introduction to Shibori: A Brief History

Shibori, an ancient Japanese art form, is a technique that dates back over a thousand years, with its origins deeply rooted in Japan's rich textile history. The term *Shibori* comes from the Japanese verb *shiboru*, meaning "to wring," "to squeeze," or "to press." These verbs perfectly encapsulate the method of creating intricate designs on fabric through the manipulation of cloth before dyeing. Shibori artisans fold, twist, tie, stitch, or compress the fabric, creating a physical resist that prevents the dye from fully penetrating, resulting in unique and beautiful patterns.

Historically, Shibori was used as an affordable way to decorate fabric for those who couldn't afford expensive, elaborately woven textiles. In the 8th century, the art form gained popularity in Japan, with the ruling class and commoners alike appreciating the patterns created through Shibori techniques. One of the earliest records of Shibori can be found in the 8th-century document, the *Nara period*, which showcased fabrics dyed using this technique. These fabrics were initially dyed with indigo, a color that became synonymous with Shibori due to its deep, striking contrast with white, creating mesmerizing patterns.

As time passed, the craft of Shibori developed and grew in complexity. During the Edo period (1603-1868), it became a sophisticated art form, with artisans developing various techniques to create more intricate and dynamic designs. Regional styles of Shibori emerged, with each region of Japan adding its own unique twist to the craft. Some areas were known for using specific materials, while others developed signature techniques. Shibori remained a popular art form, particularly in areas like Arimatsu and Narumi, where the technique was passed down from generation to generation.

Cultural Significance of Shibori in Japan

Shibori holds a special place in Japanese culture. Its beauty and versatility made it an essential part of daily life, and it was used to create everything from kimonos and garments to decorative household items. The patterns formed by Shibori are not just aesthetic; they carry symbolic meanings and reflect the artisan's creativity, skill, and connection to nature.

Shibori is deeply connected to the Japanese aesthetic principle of *wabi-sabi*, which celebrates beauty in imperfection, transience, and the natural flow of life. Unlike mass-produced fabrics, Shibori is handmade, and each piece is entirely unique. The subtle variations in patterns, the unevenness of the dye, and the organic shapes created by the resist technique exemplify *wabi-sabi* and are embraced as part of the fabric's beauty.

Furthermore, many traditional Shibori patterns hold cultural significance, representing different aspects of life in Japan. For example, the *Kumo* (spider web) pattern symbolizes strength, protection, and the connection between life's many strands, while the *Kanoko* (fawn) pattern is associated with innocence and new beginnings, mimicking the spots on a baby deer.

Artisans would often tailor their designs for specific seasons or life events, adding deeper meaning to the fabrics. In the case of kimonos, the patterns and colors chosen through Shibori might indicate the wearer's social status, the occasion, or even the time of year, as Japanese culture places great importance on aligning fashion with seasonal changes.

Today, Shibori is still cherished in Japan, not only as a traditional craft but as an art form that transcends its cultural roots. Its influence can be seen in contemporary fashion, textiles, and design. Japanese artisans continue to practice and innovate within the craft, keeping the spirit of Shibori alive while also adapting it to modern sensibilities. The town of Arimatsu remains a hub for Shibori artisans, where workshops and festivals celebrate the history and future of this intricate art.

Shibori vs. Tie-Dye: Understanding the Differences

At first glance, Shibori may seem similar to tie-dye, particularly the Western version popularized in the 1960s during the counterculture movement. Both techniques rely on the basic principle of resist-dyeing, where parts of the fabric are manipulated to resist dye penetration, creating patterns. However, while tie-dye and Shibori share some commonalities, they are fundamentally different in their execution, cultural background, and the results they produce.

1. Historical and Cultural Context: Shibori is a deeply traditional art form with roots in Japanese culture, having been practiced for over a millennium. It was a refined craft used to create garments like kimonos for both everyday and ceremonial use. The cultural reverence for Shibori in Japan also means that it has a spiritual and symbolic component, reflecting the artisan's connection to nature and their personal artistry.

On the other hand, tie-dye as it is known in the West gained mainstream popularity in the 1960s as part of the counterculture movement. Western tie-dye, while still an art form, is often seen as a more casual, DIY craft that became a symbol of individuality, peace, and freedom during the hippie movement. Its cultural connotations in the West differ significantly from the traditional artistry seen in Shibori.

2. Techniques: While both Shibori and tie-dye involve resist-dyeing techniques, Shibori employs a far more intricate and varied set of methods. Shibori artisans use techniques like stitching, folding, pleating, and wrapping to create detailed patterns. Some methods, such as *Nui Shibori* (stitched resist), require painstaking hand-sewing to achieve delicate, repeating designs. *Arashi Shibori*, where fabric is tightly wrapped around a pole and then dyed, creates a distinctive diagonal pattern that is characteristic of Japanese textile design.

Western tie-dye, on the other hand, usually involves simpler processes such as folding or crumpling the fabric, tying it with rubber bands or string, and applying dye to create spirals, bullseyes, or random bursts of color. While tie-dye can produce vibrant, bold designs, the approach is often less structured compared to the meticulous methods of Shibori.

3. Patterns and Results: Shibori's patterns are typically more subtle, organic, and controlled, often utilizing negative space (undyed portions of the fabric) to create visual balance and harmony. The patterns in Shibori are influenced by the precise techniques used to manipulate the fabric, and the finished results are usually more delicate and sophisticated. Shibori also embraces the beauty of natural, indigo-dyed textiles, where the deep blues and whites of the dye create an elegant contrast.

Tie-dye, in contrast, is known for its bold, kaleidoscopic patterns, often featuring bright and varied colors. The focus is less on precise patterns and more on the joyful unpredictability of the design, resulting in eye-catching, colorful swirls, spirals, and blotches. While this spontaneity is one of tie-dye's appeals, the art of Shibori is more structured, focusing on careful technique to achieve the desired effect.

4. Material and Dye Use: Shibori traditionally utilizes natural fabrics such as silk, cotton, or hemp, and many artisans stick to natural indigo dye. Indigo is prized for its deep blue hues and has a long history of use in Japan. The process of dyeing with natural indigo is labor-intensive, as the dye must be carefully prepared, and the fabric is often dipped multiple times to achieve the desired shade.

In Western tie-dye, synthetic dyes like Procion MX are commonly used, allowing for a wide variety of vibrant colors. These dyes can be easily mixed and applied, often directly onto the fabric using squirt bottles or sponges, making the process quicker and more accessible for casual crafters.

While both Shibori and tie-dye involve resist-dyeing techniques, the depth of history, complexity of techniques, and the nature of the patterns produced by Shibori set it apart as a highly revered and intricate art form. Tie-dye, on the other hand, remains a fun, expressive, and accessible craft with its own distinct charm. Understanding these differences enhances the appreciation for the traditional artistry of Shibori while still celebrating the creative freedom that tie-dye offers.

CHAPTER TWO

TOOLS AND MATERIALS

The beauty of Shibori lies in its simplicity, but behind that simplicity is a deliberate choice of materials and tools. To master the art of Shibori, it's essential to understand the importance of the textiles used, the equipment required for manipulation, and the types of dyes that bring the patterns to life. This chapter will guide you through selecting the best fabrics, acquiring the right tools, and making informed decisions on dye types to ensure that your Shibori creations achieve their full potential.

Fabrics: Choosing the Best Textiles for Shibori

In Shibori, the fabric you use plays a pivotal role in the final outcome. Different fabrics react differently to dye and manipulation, so choosing the right textile is crucial to achieving the desired pattern and aesthetic. The key to selecting fabric for Shibori is to focus on natural fibers, as they absorb dye better and allow for more vibrant, intricate patterns.

1. **Cotton:** Cotton is one of the most popular fabrics for Shibori, particularly for beginners. It is affordable, widely available, and easy to work

with. Cotton's natural fibers take up dye well, allowing for rich and consistent color saturation. Additionally, cotton's relatively smooth texture means that the resist techniques, such as folding, binding, and stitching, result in sharp and well-defined patterns.

When choosing cotton for Shibori, opt for tightly woven fabrics like muslin or broadcloth. These fabrics hold resistance patterns more effectively, ensuring the dye doesn't bleed too much into the bound areas, resulting in clearer lines and shapes. Cotton is also great for making functional items like table linens, pillows, and clothing.

2. **Silk:** For a more luxurious and delicate Shibori project, silk is an excellent choice. Silk fibers are finer and more absorbent than cotton, making them perfect for achieving subtle color gradients and more intricate designs. When dyed, silk reflects light beautifully, adding a soft sheen to the finished fabric, which enhances the overall aesthetic.

However, silk can be more challenging to work with compared to cotton due to its delicate nature. Care must be taken during the folding, stitching, and binding process to avoid damaging the fabric. Additionally, silk tends to hold onto dye for longer, so fewer dye dips may be needed to achieve the desired color intensity.

Silk is ideal for Shibori scarves, wraps, and other fashion accessories where the fabric's softness and sheen can be fully appreciated.

3. **Linen:** Linen, another natural fiber, is a great option for Shibori due to its strength and durability. It offers a crisp texture that holds resist patterns well, producing sharp and well-defined lines. Linen's coarser texture, however, creates a more rustic and organic look compared to cotton or silk.

    The natural inherent texture of linen can add interesting depth to Shibori patterns. It tends to wrinkle easily, so binding or stitching must be done carefully to avoid unintentional creases. Linen's ability to absorb and hold dye is impressive, resulting in vibrant colors. This makes linen perfect for home décor items such as curtains, tablecloths, or wall hangings, where its natural, earthy feel can complement any space.

4. **Hemp:** Hemp is a sustainable and eco-friendly fabric choice for Shibori. Similar to linen, it has a coarser texture, giving the finished product a raw, natural look. Hemp is durable and strong, making it ideal for creating items that require

longevity, such as bags, upholstery, or large-scale art pieces. Like other natural fibers, hemp takes dye well, though its slightly uneven texture can lead to more organic, less uniform patterns.

Working with hemp in Shibori may require extra care in the folding and binding process due to its stiffness. However, the results are often unique, with a rustic charm that stands out among more polished fabrics.

5. **Rayon:** Rayon, though technically semi-synthetic, is made from natural cellulose fibers and behaves much like cotton or silk in the dyeing process. It's soft, smooth, and drapes well, making it an excellent choice for fashion applications like scarves, skirts, or blouses. Rayon absorbs dye readily, producing deep, rich colors, but it can be delicate, so care is needed when folding, pleating, or binding.

6. **Wool:** Wool can also be used for Shibori, although it presents some challenges. Wool fibers are thick and hold resist patterns well, but they are more likely to shrink when exposed to heat or moisture. To prevent damage, it's important to avoid high-temperature dye baths and agitation during the dyeing process. Wool absorbs dye unevenly, creating interesting

texture variations, which can be appealing for certain artistic effects. Wool Shibori works well for projects like scarves, shawls, and home accessories.

Essential Tools and Equipment

In addition to selecting the right fabric, Shibori requires certain tools and equipment to manipulate the cloth, create resistance patterns, and apply the dye. Here's a breakdown of the essentials:

1. **Binding Materials:**
    - **String or Twine:** Used for binding, tying, and creating resist points on the fabric. The tension of the string or twine determines how much dye penetrates the fabric. Cotton twine is preferable, as it doesn't stretch too much and creates defined lines. For tighter patterns, thicker string or twine can be used to prevent dye from seeping into the bound areas.
    - **Rubber Bands:** These are commonly used in tie-dye but can also be used in Shibori. They are ideal for beginners because they are easy to work with and provide a tight grip on the fabric. However, rubber bands can be less precise than

string and may result in less detailed patterns.
- **Clamps and Blocks:** Essential for *Itajime Shibori* (clamped resist), these are used to sandwich the fabric between two rigid objects like wooden blocks, which prevent the dye from reaching certain parts of the fabric. The shape of the blocks directly influences the pattern.

2. **Needles and Thread:**
    - Used for *Nui Shibori* (stitched resist), needles and thread help create intricate patterns by gathering the fabric with running stitches. When pulled tight, these stitches compress the fabric and act as a resist. The finer the thread and more delicate the stitching, the more detailed the final pattern will be.

3. **Poles and Pipes:**
    - For *Arashi Shibori* (pole-wrapped), you will need poles or PVC pipes around which the fabric is wrapped tightly before dyeing. This method creates diagonal patterns reminiscent of rain streaks. Poles of different widths can be used to achieve different effects.

4. **Buckets and Basins:**

- A large container is needed to hold the dye bath. Plastic or stainless steel buckets work best, as they resist staining and corrosion. You will also need smaller containers for rinsing or preparing dye mixtures.

5. **Gloves and Apron:**
    - Protecting your skin is crucial when working with dyes. Gloves are necessary to prevent stains or chemical reactions with the dye. An apron or old clothing will protect your garments from splashes or spills.

6. **Measuring Cups and Spoons:**
    - Precision is key in dyeing. Measuring cups and spoons ensure that you use the right amount of dye, fixatives, and other chemicals, resulting in consistent and repeatable outcomes.

7. **Dyeing Rack:**
    - A rack allows the fabric to drip dry after being removed from the dye bath. It's important for ensuring that excess dye drips off, preventing unintended stains or marks on the fabric.

Types of Dyes: Natural vs. Synthetic

Choosing the right dye is essential to achieving the desired look for your Shibori project. There are two main categories of dye: natural and synthetic. Each has its own advantages, drawbacks, and aesthetic effects.

1. **Natural Dyes:**
    - **Overview:** Natural dyes are derived from plants, minerals, and other organic materials. These dyes have been used for centuries in Shibori and other traditional dyeing techniques. Natural dyes are favored by artisans who prioritize eco-friendly and sustainable practices. Some of the most common natural dyes include indigo, madder (red), and cochineal (purple).
    - **Indigo:** One of the most iconic and commonly used dyes in Shibori is indigo. Derived from the indigo plant, it creates deep, rich shades of blue that range from pale sky blue to midnight navy, depending on how many times the fabric is dipped into the dye. The natural dyeing process with indigo is unique because it requires oxidation, meaning the fabric must be exposed to air after dipping to develop the color.

- **Advantages:** Natural dyes are biodegradable and non-toxic, making them a more environmentally friendly option. They produce softer, more muted tones that give the fabric a timeless, organic look. Additionally, natural dyes can create complex, uneven color variations that add depth and character to the fabric.
- **Challenges:** Natural dyes can be more difficult to work with because they require longer preparation times, and they may fade more quickly than synthetic dyes. They also need mordants (fixatives) like alum or iron to ensure the dye adheres to the fabric and doesn't wash out over time.

2. **Synthetic Dyes:**
    - **Overview:** Synthetic dyes are chemically produced and offer a wide range of vibrant, bold colors that are more predictable and consistent than natural dyes. Procion MX dyes, for example, are a popular choice for Shibori because they are easy to use and bond well with natural fibers like cotton.
    - **Advantages:** Synthetic dyes are more readily available and offer a broad

spectrum of colors that natural dyes cannot always achieve. They are also more colorfast, meaning the colors tend to be longer-lasting and less prone to fading. Additionally, synthetic dyes are often easier to use, requiring fewer steps and less time compared to natural dyes.
- **Challenges:** The downside to synthetic dyes is that they can be harmful to the environment due to their chemical composition. They may also pose risks to health if not handled properly. Proper disposal of synthetic dye waste is crucial to minimize environmental damage.

CHAPTER THREE
TRADITIONAL SHIBORI TECHNIQUE

Shibori is an ancient Japanese dyeing art that encompasses a range of techniques, each with its unique method of fabric manipulation and resulting patterns. These techniques create intricate designs that range from delicate, subtle patterns to bold, eye-catching motifs. In this chapter, we will explore six of the most well-known traditional Shibori techniques: Kanoko, Miura, Kumo, Nui, Arashi, and Itajime Shibori. Each method brings its own character to the fabric, offering a variety of creative possibilities for any Shibori artist.

Kanoko (Bound) Shibori

Kanoko Shibori is the technique that most closely resembles what many in the West know as "tie-dye." It involves binding sections of fabric with string or thread to create small resist points that prevent the dye from reaching certain areas, resulting in circular or dot-like patterns.

The Process:

- **Binding:** In Kanoko Shibori, small sections of fabric are pinched and bound tightly with thread or twine. The bound sections will resist the dye, creating patterns in the shape of rings or dots. The tighter the binding, the more defined the pattern.
- **Variations:** The size of the bound sections and the tightness of the binding can be varied to produce different effects. Larger bound sections will result in wider rings, while smaller sections create more delicate patterns. If the fabric is folded before binding, the rings can form repeating geometric patterns.

Patterns and Aesthetics:

- Kanoko Shibori typically produces circular patterns, ranging from small dots to larger, more elaborate shapes. The patterns are often irregular, giving the design an organic and playful feel.
- By strategically placing the bindings, you can create complex motifs such as flowers or abstract shapes, which add a unique visual interest to the fabric.

Applications:

- Kanoko Shibori is often used for fabrics intended for clothing, such as scarves or garments. The delicate, dotted patterns created by this technique make it perfect for soft, flowing fabrics like silk or cotton.

Miura (Looped) Shibori

Miura Shibori, or looped Shibori, is one of the simplest and fastest Shibori techniques, making it ideal for beginners. This method does not require stitching or tight binding but instead involves a simple looping process, which results in soft, flowing patterns.

The Process:

- **Looping:** The fabric is gathered in small sections using a hook or needle. Instead of being tied or bound tightly, the fabric is looped with thread, leaving it loose. The loose loops allow the dye to seep into the fabric but not evenly, creating a soft, undulating pattern.
- **Tension Control:** The key to Miura Shibori is controlling the tension in the loops. Loosely looped areas will absorb more dye, while tighter loops will resist the dye, creating a contrast between the dyed and undyed sections.

Patterns and Aesthetics:

- Miura Shibori produces fluid, wave-like patterns with a softer, more organic appearance than Kanoko Shibori. The loose nature of the loops allows for a more dynamic and less structured design.
- The patterns often resemble ripples in water, making this technique ideal for creating calming, natural designs.

Applications:

- Miura Shibori is great for larger projects like home textiles (curtains, bedspreads) or wearable art. The gentle, flowing patterns make it perfect for casual, natural looks in both fashion and décor.

Kumo (Spider Web) Shibori

Kumo Shibori, or spider web Shibori, is a binding technique that creates intricate, web-like patterns. This technique is known for its ability to produce delicate, radial designs that resemble a spider web.

The Process:

- **Binding:** In Kumo Shibori, small objects (like stones, beads, or buttons) are placed on the fabric, and the fabric is then tightly bound around

these objects with string or thread. Alternatively, fabric can be folded in tight pleats and bound at intervals.
- **Creating Radial Patterns:** The binding creates a resist area where the dye cannot penetrate, resulting in a radiating pattern once the fabric is dyed and the binding removed. The key to this technique is binding the fabric as tightly as possible to prevent dye from seeping into the bound areas.

Patterns and Aesthetics:

- Kumo Shibori typically creates circular, web-like patterns with fine lines radiating out from the center. The resulting designs are highly detailed and can resemble anything from spider webs to sunbursts or mandalas.
- The pattern's intensity can be controlled by adjusting the size of the bound sections or using objects of different shapes and sizes.

Applications:

- Kumo Shibori is particularly striking on smaller projects such as scarves, handkerchiefs, or accessories. It can also be used for accent pieces in larger works like tapestries or wall hangings, where the intricate web pattern becomes a focal point.

Nui (Stitched) Shibori

Nui Shibori is one of the most complex Shibori techniques, as it involves hand-stitching the fabric before dyeing. The stitches are used to create intricate resist patterns, which can range from geometric shapes to freeform designs.

The Process:

- **Stitching:** In Nui Shibori, designs are first drawn or imagined onto the fabric, and then running stitches are sewn along these designs using strong thread. Once the stitching is complete, the thread is pulled tight, gathering the fabric into pleats and creating resist areas.
- **Binding the Stitching:** After the fabric is gathered, the stitched areas are often bound further with string or twine to enhance the resist effect.

Patterns and Aesthetics:

- Nui Shibori produces highly detailed, controlled patterns. The use of stitches allows for more precision than techniques like binding or

clamping. Common patterns include waves, concentric circles, or even more intricate designs like flowers or animals.
- The resulting patterns are sharp and clearly defined, with crisp lines and shapes that can be much more intricate than other Shibori techniques.

Applications:

- Nui Shibori is perfect for high-detail projects where intricate design is paramount. This technique works well for decorative pieces like wall art or luxury clothing items, where the precision of the pattern can be fully appreciated.

Arashi (Pole-Wrapped) Shibori

Arashi Shibori, or pole-wrapped Shibori, creates beautiful, diagonal patterns that resemble rain streaks. "Arashi" means "storm" in Japanese, referring to the flowing, linear designs this method produces.

The Process:

- **Wrapping the Fabric:** In Arashi Shibori, the fabric is wrapped diagonally around a pole or cylinder (such as a PVC pipe or bamboo rod). Once wrapped, the fabric is bound tightly with

string or twine to secure it in place. The fabric may also be scrunched down the pole to create more irregular patterns.
- **Dye Application:** The dye is then applied while the fabric is still on the pole. Because the fabric is tightly bound, the dye can only penetrate the areas that are not under the string or twine, resulting in diagonal, streaked patterns.

Patterns and Aesthetics:

- Arashi Shibori produces fluid, linear patterns that are reminiscent of rainfall or wind blowing through grass. The lines can be straight and regular or wavy and irregular, depending on how tightly the fabric is wrapped and how much it is scrunched.
- The patterns can be fine and delicate or bold and striking, depending on the size of the pole and the tightness of the binding.

Applications:

- Arashi Shibori is often used for fashion textiles, such as scarves, dresses, or jackets, where the flowing diagonal patterns can enhance the drape of the fabric. It is also great for larger pieces like curtains or tablecloths, where the bold, linear patterns can make a strong visual statement.

Itajime (Clamped) Shibori

Itajime Shibori is a clamping technique that creates geometric, symmetrical patterns. The fabric is folded and then sandwiched between two blocks (typically wood or acrylic), which are then clamped tightly together to resist the dye.

The Process:

- **Folding the Fabric:** The fabric is folded multiple times, either in a simple accordion fold or in more complex geometric folds. The more folds, the more intricate the resulting pattern.
- **Clamping:** Once folded, the fabric is placed between two rigid blocks, and clamps are applied to hold the fabric in place. The blocks prevent the dye from reaching certain areas of the fabric, creating a resist pattern. The shape of the blocks and the way the fabric is folded determine the final design.
- **Dyeing:** The dye is applied to the fabric while it is clamped. When the clamps are removed after dyeing, the result is a symmetrical, repeating pattern.

Patterns and Aesthetics:

- Itajime Shibori typically produces geometric patterns, such as squares, triangles, or diamonds, depending on how the fabric is folded and clamped. The resulting designs are sharp and symmetrical, offering a modern and structured look compared to the more organic patterns of other Shibori techniques.
- The sharp contrast between the dyed and undyed areas creates a striking, graphic effect that can be bold or subtle, depending on the colors used.

Applications:

- Itajime Shibori is ideal for creating textiles with a modern, graphic look. It is often used for items like pillow covers, table linens, or wall hangings. The geometric patterns can also be used for fashion accessories or garments, where the bold design can stand out against simpler fabrics.

CHAPTER FOUR
MODERN INTERPRETATIONS OF SHIBORI

Shibori, though deeply rooted in traditional Japanese craftsmanship, has evolved over time to accommodate contemporary tastes, styles, and innovations. The ancient techniques have given rise to new methods, patterns, and applications, making Shibori a versatile and timeless art form. In this chapter, we will explore how modern artisans and designers experiment with color, introduce contemporary patterns and designs, and blend traditional techniques with modern approaches to create fresh interpretations of this ancient craft.

Experimenting with Colors

While traditional Shibori typically uses indigo as the primary dye, modern interpretations have expanded the color palette significantly. Artists and designers today experiment with various dyes, both natural and synthetic, allowing for a vibrant array of hues and shades.

Expanding Beyond Indigo:

- **Multicolor Shibori:** One of the most notable innovations in modern Shibori is the use of multiple colors. By applying dyes in different stages or blending them during the dyeing process, artisans can create intricate, multicolor designs. This adds a dynamic visual quality to the fabric, elevating the traditional monochromatic look of Shibori into a more playful and contemporary art form.
- **Ombre and Gradient Effects:** Artists have begun experimenting with gradient or ombre dyeing techniques to create soft transitions between colors. By immersing the fabric in dye at different intervals or gradually pulling it out of the dye bath, it is possible to create a smooth gradient that blends one color into another. This adds depth and dimension to the fabric, making it visually striking and perfect for modern textiles like fashion garments or home décor.
- **Layering Colors:** Modern Shibori also embraces color layering, where fabrics are dyed multiple times with different colors. For example, a fabric might first be dyed with a light color, then bound and dyed again with a darker color. This layering technique allows for complex, layered patterns where colors interact with each other, producing rich, multidimensional effects.

Custom Color Palettes:

- **Personalized Color Choices:** Contemporary Shibori artisans often work with custom color palettes, tailored to specific design needs. By using a mix of muted tones, pastel shades, or bold and vivid colors, designers can create fabrics that match contemporary fashion and interior design trends. This allows for endless personalization and experimentation with modern aesthetics while maintaining the essence of the Shibori process.

The Influence of Fabric Type on Color:

- **Fabrics and Dye Absorption:** Different fabrics absorb dyes in unique ways, adding another layer of complexity to modern Shibori. Synthetic fabrics often react differently than natural ones, producing unexpected variations in color intensity and pattern definition. Modern artists leverage these differences to create unique effects that may not have been achievable with traditional cotton, silk, or hemp.

Contemporary Patterns and Designs

In modern Shibori, the introduction of new patterns and creative designs has further expanded the possibilities of this technique. While the traditional geometric and organic patterns remain popular, today's artists push the boundaries by incorporating more complex designs, abstract concepts, and even digital technology.

Asymmetry and Abstract Designs:

- **Breaking the Symmetry:** Traditional Shibori often emphasizes symmetry, with repeating geometric patterns created through folding, binding, or clamping. However, modern interpretations frequently break away from this structure, embracing asymmetry and organic, freeform designs. The resulting patterns feel more fluid and spontaneous, reflecting the unpredictable nature of hand-dyeing and the creativity of the artist.
- **Abstract Art on Fabric:** Modern Shibori artists often use the technique to create abstract art, where the patterns may not adhere to a recognizable form. Instead of aiming for specific shapes like circles or diamonds, these designs focus on texture, movement, and the interplay of light and dark areas on the fabric. This abstract approach gives the fabric an artistic, almost painterly quality, making it suitable for high-end fashion and art installations.

Geometric Complexity:

- **Innovative Folding Techniques:** Artists today are experimenting with more intricate folding techniques to create highly complex geometric patterns. By folding the fabric in innovative ways before binding or clamping, they can produce detailed, multi-layered designs that surpass the simplicity of traditional Shibori. These patterns often have a more contemporary feel, aligning with modern aesthetics in interior design and fashion.
- **Precision and Repetition:** With advancements in technology, some modern artists have introduced tools to achieve precise repetition in their patterns. Digital stencils and laser-cut templates allow for more control over the design process, creating fabrics that have a clean, polished look. While this reduces some of the organic unpredictability of traditional Shibori, it allows for a level of intricacy and detail that would be difficult to achieve by hand.

Incorporating Nature-Inspired Designs:

- **Botanical Motifs:** In addition to abstract and geometric designs, many contemporary Shibori artists draw inspiration from nature, incorporating

botanical motifs such as leaves, flowers, and vines into their work. By using folding and binding techniques that mimic the shapes of plants or even incorporating actual leaves into the dyeing process, these artists can create patterns that evoke a connection to the natural world.
- **Water-Inspired Patterns:** Water, a fundamental element in the dyeing process, also serves as inspiration for modern Shibori designs. Ripple effects, wave-like patterns, and designs that resemble rain or streams are common in contemporary Shibori, especially in works that aim to create a sense of fluidity and movement in the fabric.

Mixing Traditional and Modern Techniques

One of the most exciting aspects of modern Shibori is the combination of ancient methods with contemporary innovations. Artists are constantly finding new ways to blend traditional hand-dyeing techniques with modern practices, creating work that pays homage to the craft's roots while pushing it forward into new territories.

Combining Multiple Shibori Techniques:

- **Layering Techniques:** Artists today often combine multiple traditional Shibori techniques to create intricate, layered designs. For example, a fabric might be first bound in the Kanoko Shibori style to create circular resist areas, and then further folded and clamped in the Itajime style to create geometric patterns within those circles. This mixing of techniques allows for highly detailed and sophisticated patterns that merge the best elements of different Shibori methods.
- **Sequential Dyeing:** In modern Shibori, it's common to see sequential dyeing processes that layer multiple dye baths using different techniques. For instance, fabric may first be dyed using the Arashi technique, then refolded and redyed using Nui Shibori. The combination of different resist methods and dye applications results in patterns that are much more complex than what can be achieved with a single technique.

Fusion with Modern Dyeing Methods:

- **Digital Enhancements:** Some modern Shibori artists incorporate digital tools and technology into their work. For example, after dyeing the fabric traditionally, they may use digital printing to add further detail or enhance the design. This

fusion of traditional handcrafting and modern technology allows for an incredible range of possibilities, blending the best of both worlds.
- **Sublimation and Heat-Transfer Printing:** Modern innovations like sublimation printing or heat-transfer methods allow Shibori-inspired designs to be applied to synthetic fabrics, expanding the range of textiles that can carry these unique patterns. While these processes may not involve the traditional resist dyeing techniques, they replicate the aesthetic of Shibori and enable mass production of Shibori-like designs for the fashion and textile industries.

Incorporating Modern Fabrics and Techniques:

- **Use of Synthetic Fabrics:** While traditional Shibori primarily focuses on natural fibers like cotton, silk, and linen, modern Shibori artists experiment with synthetic fabrics such as polyester or nylon. These fabrics often interact differently with dyes, resulting in unique textures and color effects. Combining traditional Shibori techniques with synthetic fabrics creates a contemporary twist on the classic art form.
- **Blending Shibori with Other Textile Arts:** Modern artists are also combining Shibori with

other textile arts, such as screen printing, embroidery, or block printing. These hybrid designs allow for even greater creative expression, as different techniques are layered on top of or integrated into the dyed fabric. The result is a fusion of traditional craftsmanship and modern artistry that reflects today's diverse design landscape.

CHAPTER FIVE
PREPARING THE FABRIC

The beauty and success of any Shibori project depend heavily on how well the fabric is prepared. Each step leading up to the dyeing process is crucial to achieving the desired patterns and color effects. From washing and pre-treating the fabric to folding, pleating, and binding it in intricate ways, careful preparation lays the foundation for a successful Shibori design. This chapter delves into the essential steps for fabric preparation and offers techniques and tips to help you achieve the perfect resistance for your Shibori projects.

Washing and Pre-treating the Fabric

Before you begin folding and binding your fabric, it's important to properly clean and prepare it. This ensures that the fabric can absorb the dye evenly, leading to vibrant colors and well-defined patterns.

Why Pre-Washing is Important:

- **Removing Sizing and Impurities:** Many fabrics, especially cotton and linen, come coated with a substance known as "sizing." This is a finish added during the manufacturing process to give the fabric a crisp, new appearance. However, sizing can prevent the dye from properly penetrating the fabric. Washing the fabric helps to remove sizing, dust, and other impurities, ensuring that the dye takes to the fabric more effectively.

- **Opening the Fabric's Fibers:** Washing the fabric softens its fibers, making them more receptive to dye. When fibers are open and ready to absorb the dye, the resulting colors will be richer and more intense. This is particularly important for Shibori, where you want strong contrasts between the dyed and resisted areas.

Best Practices for Washing:

- **Use a Mild Detergent:** Choose a mild, non-toxic detergent to wash your fabric. Avoid fabric softeners or harsh chemicals, as they can affect the way the fabric interacts with the dye.
- **Cold or Warm Water:** Washing the fabric in cold or warm water is generally sufficient for removing sizing and opening the fibers. If the fabric is particularly dirty or coated with heavy sizing, you may want to use warm water for a deeper clean.
- **Drying:** After washing, air-dry your fabric until it's slightly damp. Some Shibori artists prefer to fold and bind the fabric while it's still a bit moist,

as this can make the fabric easier to manipulate. Others prefer the fabric to be fully dry. Experiment to see which method works best for your technique.

Pre-Treatment for Natural Dyes:

- **Mordanting the Fabric:** If you're using natural dyes, you may need to treat the fabric with a mordant before dyeing. A mordant is a substance that helps the dye bond to the fabric more effectively, resulting in longer-lasting colors. Common mordants include alum, tannin, and iron. The specific mordant you use will depend on the type of dye and fabric you're working with.
- **Soaking the Fabric:** After mordanting, it's often recommended to soak the fabric in water for several hours or overnight before beginning the dyeing process. This helps the mordant fully penetrate the fibers and prepares the fabric for even dye absorption.

Folding, Pleating, and Binding Techniques

Once your fabric is clean and pre-treated, it's time to start shaping it for the dyeing process. How you fold, pleat, and bind the fabric determines the pattern that will emerge after dyeing. Shibori offers an incredible range of folding techniques, each producing a unique resistance and design.

Folding Techniques:

- **Accordion Fold:** The accordion fold, also known as fan folding, is one of the simplest and most versatile techniques. To achieve this fold, you simply fold the fabric back and forth in a zig-zag pattern, much like you would when folding a fan. The tighter the folds, the more distinct the resist lines will be. The accordion fold is often combined with clamping or binding to create geometric patterns.
- **Triangle Fold:** For more intricate designs, the triangle fold is a popular choice. Start by folding the fabric into an accordion, then fold it again into a series of triangles. This technique creates complex geometric patterns, especially when combined with clamps or stitched resist techniques.
- **Rectangular and Square Folds:** Folding the fabric into squares or rectangles before clamping or binding can produce grids or checkerboard patterns. This is commonly used in Itajime Shibori, where the folded fabric is clamped

between two boards to create symmetrical designs.

Pleating Techniques:

- **Fine Pleating:** Fine pleating involves tightly pleating the fabric into small, precise folds. The closer the pleats, the more detailed the resulting pattern will be. This technique is often used in Nui (stitched) Shibori to create intricate linear designs.
- **Loose Pleating:** If you're looking for a more organic, wavy pattern, you can use looser pleating. Loose pleats create larger areas of resistance, leading to broader swaths of undyed fabric and a more relaxed, flowing design.

Binding Techniques:

- **Simple Binding:** The most basic binding technique involves wrapping rubber bands, twine, or string tightly around the folded fabric. The pressure from the binding prevents the dye from reaching the fabric, creating resist patterns. The tighter the binding, the more defined the resist areas will be. Simple binding is most often used in Kanoko (bound) Shibori to create circular or spot-like patterns.

- **Knotting:** Knotting is another common binding technique. By tying knots directly into the fabric, you create a natural resistance where the fabric bunches together. This technique is often used to create organic, irregular patterns. The tighter the knots, the larger the resist area will be.
- **Clamping:** Clamping is a key feature of Itajime Shibori. After folding the fabric into squares or triangles, wooden boards or other objects are clamped on either side of the fabric. These objects create a resist where they block the dye, resulting in symmetrical patterns. You can experiment with different shapes of boards or objects to create a wide variety of designs.

Tips for Achieving Consistent Patterns:

- **Tightness Matters:** The tighter you fold, pleat, and bind the fabric, the crisper and more defined your resist lines will be. Loose folding or binding allows more dye to seep into the fabric, resulting in softer, more diffused patterns.
- **Experiment with Spacing:** The way you space out your folds and bindings affects the overall design. Tighter, closely packed folds will produce more intricate patterns, while wider spacing creates larger, more open designs.

- **Test Small Samples:** Before committing to a full piece, it's a good idea to test your folding and binding techniques on small samples. This allows you to see how the fabric will respond to the dye and adjust your method accordingly.
- **Varying Pressures:** Try varying the pressure of your binding. Some areas can be tightly bound for strong resistance, while others can be bound more loosely for a subtler effect. This adds variation and depth to your design.

Achieving the Perfect Resist: Methods and Tips

Resist dyeing is the essence of Shibori, where parts of the fabric are protected from the dye to create patterns. Understanding the methods and techniques for achieving a strong resistance is key to producing well-defined, beautiful designs.

Ensuring a Strong Resist:

- **Binding Pressure:** The tighter the fabric is bound, the less dye will penetrate those areas, resulting in a strong, clear resist. However, be mindful not to bind too tightly if working with delicate fabrics, as this could cause tearing or distortion.

- **Multiple Layers of Binding:** In some cases, applying multiple layers of binding or clamping can create an even stronger resistance. For example, after folding and binding the fabric, you might add another layer of string or clamps to enhance the resist effect.
- **Using Resist Materials:** Wax or paste resist can be used alongside binding techniques to enhance the resist areas. Applying wax to certain parts of the fabric before folding or binding can create a two-tiered resist effect, adding more complexity to the pattern.

Tips for Achieving Even Results:

- **Consistent Folding and Binding:** One of the keys to achieving even patterns is consistency. When folding the fabric, try to maintain even, straight folds. Likewise, make sure your bindings are spaced evenly to ensure a balanced pattern.
- **Control Dye Application:** For the most precise results, carefully control how you apply the dye. Immersing the fabric too quickly or unevenly can cause the dye to seep into the resist areas. Consider dipping the fabric slowly, allowing the dye to penetrate in a controlled manner.
- **Work in Stages:** If you're using multiple dye colors, work in stages. Apply one color at a time,

allowing the fabric to dry in between, before adding the next color. This layered approach ensures that your resist areas stay intact throughout the dyeing process.

Common Resist Problems and Solutions:

- **Leaking Dye:** If you notice that dye is leaking into areas that should remain resisted, check the tightness of your bindings or folds. If necessary, rebind the fabric more tightly or add an additional layer of resist.
- **Uneven Dye Absorption:** Uneven patterns can sometimes occur if the fabric is folded or bound unevenly, or if the dye is applied inconsistently. To avoid this, double-check your folding and binding process before dyeing, and ensure that the dye bath is evenly mixed.
- **Fading Patterns:** If your resist areas are fading or not as vibrant as you expected, it could be due to the type of dye or fabric you're using. Natural dyes, for example, can sometimes produce subtler results than synthetic dyes. Experiment with different fabrics and dye types to find the combination that produces the strongest resistance for your project.

CHAPTER SIX
DYEING TECHNIQUES

Dyeing is the heart of the Shibori process, where the magic truly begins. The way you apply the dye transforms the folded and bound fabric into a masterpiece of color and pattern. This chapter explores various dyeing techniques, from full immersion dyeing to creating gradients and blending colors. Each method offers a unique way to express creativity and personalize your Shibori projects.

Immersion Dyeing: Full Coverage Techniques

Immersion dyeing is one of the most common and traditional methods in Shibori. It involves submerging the fabric entirely in a dye bath, allowing for full coverage of the dye across the fabric. This technique is straightforward but can result in intricate patterns depending on how the fabric is folded, bound, or resisted.

Steps for Immersion Dyeing:

1. **Prepare the Dye Bath:** Follow the instructions for your chosen dye (natural or synthetic) to prepare the dye bath. Ensure the dye is evenly

dissolved in the water, and the temperature is optimal for the fabric you're using.

2. **Submerge the Fabric:** Place your folded, bound, or clamped fabric into the dye bath. For even color absorption, ensure that the fabric is fully submerged. If you're working with larger pieces of fabric, you may need to use a stirring stick to move the fabric around, allowing the dye to reach all areas.

3. **Time in the Dye Bath:** The time you leave the fabric in the dye bath affects the intensity of the color. A longer immersion will result in a deeper, more saturated color, while a shorter immersion will give you a lighter shade. Natural dyes often require more time in the bath compared to synthetic dyes.

4. **Rinse and Unbind:** Once the fabric has absorbed the dye to your satisfaction, carefully remove it from the dye bath. Rinse the fabric in cold water until the water runs clear to remove any excess dye. Finally, unbind or unclamp the fabric to reveal the pattern.

Achieving Full Coverage:

- **Even Submersion:** Ensure that the fabric is fully submerged to avoid unwanted dye spots or

uneven patches. Stirring the fabric during the process can help achieve even coverage.
- **Multiple Dips:** For darker or more intense colors, consider dipping the fabric multiple times, allowing it to dry slightly between dips. This builds up the color gradually and reduces the risk of uneven dyeing.

Patterns from Immersion Dyeing:

The patterns that emerge from immersion dyeing depend entirely on how the fabric was folded, pleated, or bound. The resist areas, where the dye couldn't penetrate, will remain undyed, creating the beautiful contrast characteristic of Shibori.

Dip Dyeing: Creating Gradients and Ombres

Dip dyeing offers an elegant and simple way to create gradients, ombre effects, or transitions between colors. This method is perfect for achieving soft, flowing patterns that blend one color into another, creating a sophisticated look on fabrics.

Steps for Dip Dyeing:

1. **Prepare the Dye Bath:** Mix the dye as you would for immersion dyeing, ensuring it is fully dissolved and at the correct temperature.

2. **Dipping the Fabric:** Instead of submerging the fabric completely, dip only a portion of it into the dye bath. Hold the fabric for a few minutes to allow the dye to absorb.
3. **Gradual Dipping:** To create a gradient effect, slowly lower more of the fabric into the dye bath in small increments, leaving the previous section in the dye longer than the new section. This results in a gradual change in color intensity from light to dark.
4. **Layering Colors:** For a multi-color ombre, start by dyeing one section of the fabric with a light color. After rinsing and drying, repeat the process with a darker shade, dipping the opposite end of the fabric into the new dye bath.

Tips for Smooth Gradients:

- **Slow Dipping:** The slower and more gradual the dip, the smoother the gradient. Rushing the process can create sharp lines between color transitions.
- **Layering for Intensity:** If the gradient appears too subtle, you can layer additional dye onto the same area by dipping the fabric again. This intensifies the color without harsh lines.
- **Blending Multiple Colors:** To blend two or more colors, dip one section of the fabric into one dye

bath, rinse, and then dip another section into a different dye. The overlapping area will create a third, blended color.

Ombre Patterns:

The beauty of ombre dyeing is its versatility. You can create single-color gradients that shift from light to dark, or experiment with multi-color blends to create a sunset effect or a water-like transition between colors.

Layering Dyes for Complex Effects

Layering dyes is an advanced technique that adds depth and complexity to Shibori patterns. By applying multiple layers of dye, each in a different color or shade, you can create intricate and multi-dimensional effects. This method requires patience and planning but yields stunning results.

Steps for Layering Dyes:

1. **Dye the Base Layer:** Start by applying the lightest color first. For instance, if you want to create a layered design using shades of blue and purple, dye the fabric in a light blue or a pastel tone as the base layer.
2. **Dry the Fabric:** After dyeing the first layer, allow the fabric to dry completely. This ensures that

the next layer of dye won't bleed into the base color.
3. **Re-Fold or Re-Bind:** After the base color has dried, re-fold or re-bind the fabric in a different pattern to create new resist areas. This allows you to build layers of color on top of the original design.
4. **Dye the Next Layer:** Dip the fabric into a second dye bath of a different color or a deeper shade of the same color. The new dye will only penetrate the unbound areas, layering over the previous color and adding dimension to the design.
5. **Repeat as Needed:** You can continue adding layers, each time folding or binding the fabric in new ways and using progressively darker or contrasting colors.

Tips for Successful Layering:

- **Plan Your Colors:** Start with lighter colors and work your way toward darker or more intense shades. It's difficult to layer light colors over dark, so plan your color palette accordingly.
- **Experiment with Resists:** Try using different binding techniques for each layer to create complex, overlapping patterns. For instance, you can use Kanoko Shibori for the first layer and

Kumo Shibori for the second, creating a multi-dimensional pattern.
- **Allow Drying Time:** Let each layer dry fully before adding the next. Wet fabric can cause dyes to bleed into each other, ruining the crisp lines of your design.

Overdyeing and Color Blending

Overdyeing involves dyeing a fabric that has already been dyed in one color with a second color. This technique is excellent for blending colors, correcting mistakes, or adding new dimensions to an existing design. Overdyeing can result in unexpected, rich color combinations as the original dye interacts with the new layer.

Steps for Overdyeing:

1. **Choose Your Base Fabric:** You can start with fabric that has already been dyed using any technique. Ensure the base color is light enough that the second color will show through effectively.
2. **Fold or Bind the Fabric:** Rebind the fabric using a new folding or resist technique. You can choose to leave some of the base color exposed

by using resist, or you can cover the entire fabric with the new dye.
3. **Dye the Fabric Again:** Dip the fabric into the new dye bath. The new dye will interact with the original color, blending or contrasting to create a new hue.
4. **Rinse and Unbind:** Rinse the fabric thoroughly and unbind it to reveal the layered or blended design.

Tips for Color Blending:

- **Complementary Colors:** Choose complementary or analogous colors for a harmonious blend. For example, overdyeing a light blue fabric with a green dye can result in a stunning blue-green blend.
- **Experiment with Contrasts:** For a bolder look, use contrasting colors. For instance, overdyeing yellow fabric with purple dye can create interesting, unexpected hues where the colors overlap.
- **Subtle Overdyes:** If you want a more subtle effect, choose a color that is close in shade to the original fabric. This creates a tonal effect that adds depth without being too dramatic.

Correcting Dyeing Mistakes:

Overdyeing is a great way to salvage a project that didn't turn out as expected. If a color is too light, or if the pattern is too faint, you can overdye the fabric to enhance the design. By choosing a darker or complementary color, you can breathe new life into a flawed project.

CHAPTER SEVEN

PATTERNS AND DESIGNS

The beauty of Shibori lies in the infinite variety of patterns and designs you can create through simple techniques like folding, binding, and dyeing. From precise, geometric shapes to flowing, organic patterns, Shibori offers endless creative possibilities. In this chapter, we will explore different styles of Shibori patterns, focusing on geometric precision, organic fluidity, and the balance between symmetry and asymmetry.

Geometric Patterns: Crisp Lines and Shapes

Geometric patterns in Shibori emphasize sharp lines, repeating shapes, and structured designs. These patterns are often created through precise folding, clamping, or binding techniques, resulting in a consistent, calculated pattern across the fabric. While traditional Shibori techniques tend to lean toward organic forms, geometric patterns have become a popular way to modernize and stylize the art.

Techniques for Creating Geometric Patterns:

1. **Itajime (Clamped) Shibori:** One of the best techniques for creating geometric designs is Itajime Shibori, where fabric is folded into shapes and then clamped between wooden blocks. The resist created by the blocks results in crisp, repeating shapes such as squares, triangles, or diamonds. For example, by folding fabric into accordion pleats and clamping it with rectangular blocks, you can create a pattern of symmetrical rectangles.
2. **Arashi (Pole-Wrapped) Shibori:** Arashi Shibori, which involves wrapping fabric around a pole and binding it tightly before dyeing, can also create geometric patterns. By folding the fabric before wrapping it, you can achieve angular patterns or stripes with clean, diagonal lines. The tight wrapping ensures that the resist lines are sharp and well-defined.
3. **Folding Techniques:** By folding the fabric into grids or shapes before binding, you can create geometric patterns. For example, folding the fabric into triangles and binding it in strategic places can result in tessellating triangular patterns once dyed. The key to geometric Shibori lies in the precision of your folds and the consistency of your binding.

Achieving Precision:

- **Consistent Folding:** The sharpness of the lines in geometric patterns depends on how evenly and precisely the fabric is folded. Use a ruler or other guides to ensure straight lines and uniform sections.
- **Accurate Clamping:** When using the Itajime technique, ensure that the clamping blocks are placed precisely to maintain symmetry and consistency in the pattern. The tighter the clamps, the crisper the lines will be.

Popular Geometric Designs:

- **Grid Patterns:** Simple grid patterns can be achieved by folding the fabric in squares or rectangles and using Itajime Shibori. This creates crisp, alternating squares or rectangular blocks of color and resist.
- **Diamonds and Triangles:** Folding the fabric into triangles or diamonds and clamping it with corresponding shapes produces intricate, symmetrical designs that resemble kaleidoscopic patterns.

Organic Patterns: Freeform and Nature-Inspired Designs

In contrast to the precise lines of geometric Shibori, organic patterns embrace the freeform, flowing nature of dye and resist techniques. These designs often take inspiration from the natural world, mimicking elements like water ripples, spider webs, or tree branches. Organic patterns are characterized by their fluidity, irregularity, and spontaneity.

Techniques for Creating Organic Patterns:

1. **Kumo (Spider Web) Shibori:** This technique is perfect for creating organic, radial patterns that resemble spider webs or rippling water. By tightly binding sections of fabric with thread in small, irregular bundles, you can create patterns with circular, swirling shapes. The tighter the bind, the finer the lines, while looser binds result in broader, more flowing designs.
2. **Miura (Looped) Shibori:** Miura Shibori, also known as looped binding, creates irregular, flowing patterns reminiscent of tree branches or natural forms. In this technique, you pinch sections of the fabric and loop thread around them without tying tight knots. As the fabric absorbs the dye, the loops create soft, uneven resist areas, producing a natural, organic look.
3. **Kanoko (Bound) Shibori:** Known in the West as the precursor to tie-dye, Kanoko Shibori

involves tightly binding sections of fabric with string to create resist areas. The resulting patterns are often circular and resemble the random, free-flowing shapes found in nature, like raindrops or leaves.

Achieving Natural Fluidity:

- **Loose Binding:** Organic patterns benefit from a more relaxed approach to binding and folding. Allow the fabric to take on irregular shapes rather than forcing it into strict lines. Looser binding produces more diffuse, flowing patterns.
- **Random Placement:** When creating organic designs, resist the urge to create uniformity. Placing your bindings or stitches randomly across the fabric can result in a more spontaneous, natural look.
- **Dye Flow:** Allow the dye to flow naturally through the fabric, creating unexpected color variations and blending. Organic designs thrive on the unpredictable interaction between dye and resist.

Popular Organic Designs:

- **Water Ripples:** By using loose binding techniques like Kumo Shibori, you can create

patterns that mimic the gentle, concentric ripples of water.
- **Spider Webs:** Tightly binding small sections in a circular pattern can result in delicate, web-like designs, perfect for a nature-inspired aesthetic.
- **Tree Branches:** Miura Shibori's loose, looped binding creates patterns that resemble branching trees or veins, offering an organic, earthy design.

Symmetry and Asymmetry in Shibori

One of the most interesting aspects of Shibori is the balance between symmetry and asymmetry in patterns. Symmetry can evoke a sense of order and precision, while asymmetry adds a dynamic, artistic feel. By understanding how to work with both symmetrical and asymmetrical designs, you can add variety and depth to your Shibori creations.

Symmetrical Patterns:

Symmetry is often found in geometric Shibori designs, where the folding, binding, and clamping techniques result in mirrored or repeating patterns. Symmetry brings a sense of harmony and balance to the fabric, making it visually appealing.

- **Achieving Symmetry:** To create symmetrical designs, carefully fold the fabric so that each

side mirrors the other. For example, in Itajime Shibori, folding the fabric into precise grids or shapes ensures that the resulting pattern is consistent and symmetrical.
- **Repeated Patterns:** Symmetry also comes into play when repeating a pattern across the fabric. For instance, using the same folding technique on multiple sections of fabric creates a uniform, balanced design.

Asymmetrical Patterns:

In contrast, asymmetry embraces the irregular and unexpected. Asymmetrical Shibori patterns often feel more dynamic and expressive, offering a more artistic or avant-garde aesthetic. These designs are common in organic Shibori techniques, where the natural flow of dye and resist creates unique, one-of-a-kind patterns.

- **Embracing Imperfection:** Asymmetry celebrates the irregularities and imperfections that occur naturally in the dyeing process. Loose folds, uneven bindings, and random dye application contribute to an unpredictable, artistic look.
- **Controlled Asymmetry:** While asymmetry may seem random, it can be used strategically. By placing one bold, asymmetrical design element

against a simpler background, you can create a focal point that draws the eye and adds visual interest.

Combining Symmetry and Asymmetry:

Some of the most striking Shibori designs combine both symmetry and asymmetry. For example, you might create a symmetrical pattern using Itajime Shibori but introduce asymmetry by varying the color intensity or leaving parts of the fabric undyed. This contrast between order and spontaneity can result in a balanced yet intriguing design.

CHAPTER EIGHT
POST-DYEING CARE

Once your Shibori dyeing process is complete, how you handle the fabric afterward is just as important as the dyeing itself. Proper post-dyeing care ensures that your beautiful designs stay vibrant, the dye sets permanently, and the fabric remains in excellent condition. This chapter will guide you through the crucial steps of rinsing, unwrapping, setting the dye, and post-dye treatments to finish your Shibori project with professional results.

Rinsing and Unwrapping Your Fabric

The first step after dyeing is carefully rinsing and unwrapping your fabric. The rinsing process not only removes excess dye but also prevents bleeding and keeps your patterns crisp. Unwrapping the fabric at this stage reveals the magical transformation from bound, folded material to a vibrant work of art.

Rinsing Your Fabric:

1. **Initial Rinse with Cold Water:**
    - After your dye has been allowed to set for the recommended period (usually several

hours or overnight), the fabric should first be rinsed in cold water. This helps remove the bulk of the excess dye without disturbing the resist patterns created by your bindings.
- Hold the fabric under running water until the water runs clear. The cold water rinse helps prevent the colors from bleeding too much into the un-dyed areas.

2. **Handling Bound Fabric:**
   - Be sure to keep the bindings intact during the initial rinse, as removing them too early could lead to smudging or unintended dye transfer. Rinse the fabric gently to avoid loosening the resist areas prematurely.

3. **Gradual Transition to Warm Water:**
   - Once the water starts to run clear in the cold rinse, switch to lukewarm water for a more thorough wash. This helps remove any remaining loose dye particles without causing color to bleed.

4. **Using Mild Detergent:**
   - After the initial rinse, you can introduce a mild detergent or fabric soap to help further cleanse the fabric. Ensure the detergent is dye-friendly, as harsh

chemicals can damage the fabric and dull the dye. Gently agitate the fabric in the water with detergent to fully remove excess dye.

Unwrapping the Fabric:

1. **Unbinding Carefully:**
    - Once the fabric has been thoroughly rinsed, it's time to carefully remove the bindings. Be gentle, as the fabric may still be delicate and susceptible to dye transfer. Using scissors, cut away the string, rubber bands, or thread bindings without disturbing the resist areas.
2. **Reveal the Patterns:**
    - As you slowly unwrap the fabric, you'll begin to see the intricate designs and resist patterns revealed. This moment is one of the most exciting parts of the Shibori process, where you get to see the final result of your hard work.
    - Take your time unwrapping, ensuring that you don't rush the process and risk smudging or damaging the fabric.
3. **Rinse Again (If Necessary):**
    - After unwrapping, if there are still traces of excess dye, give the fabric a final rinse

under running water to ensure the patterns are crisp and clean.

Setting the Dye: Fixatives and Techniques

To ensure that the colors in your Shibori project remain vibrant and permanent, setting the dye is crucial. Without this step, the dye may fade over time or bleed when washed. Fixatives and setting techniques help lock in the color and preserve the beauty of your designs.

Common Fixatives:

1. **Salt (For Natural Dyes):**
    - For natural dye processes, salt acts as a natural mordant or fixative. After rinsing your fabric, soaking it in a saltwater solution helps to set the dye by binding the color to the fibers.
    - Use about ¼ cup of salt per gallon of water. Soak the fabric for 30 minutes to an hour before rinsing again in cold water.
2. **Vinegar (For Acid Dyes):**
    - For synthetic or acid dyes, a vinegar bath can be used to help lock in the color. Create a solution with 1 part vinegar to 4 parts water and let the fabric soak for

about 20–30 minutes. The acidity of the vinegar helps set the dye in the fabric, especially with protein fibers like silk or wool.

3. **Commercial Dye Fixatives:**
    - Commercial dye fixatives, such as Retayne, are specifically formulated to ensure that synthetic and natural dyes remain vibrant. These products are usually available at craft or fabric stores and are mixed with water as instructed. After rinsing the fabric, it's soaked in the fixative solution, which helps maintain the dye over many washes.

Techniques for Setting the Dye:

1. **Heat Setting:**
    - Heat can be an effective way to set dyes, especially for synthetic fabrics. One method is to use an iron on medium-high heat after the fabric has dried. Iron the fabric on both sides to lock in the color. Alternatively, a clothes dryer can also be used to heat-set the dye.
2. **Steaming:**
    - Another technique to set the dye, particularly for natural dyes, is steaming.

After rinsing and drying, wrap the fabric in a clean cloth and place it in a steamer for 30 minutes to an hour. The steam helps enhance colorfastness, ensuring the dye adheres properly to the fabric.

3. **Sun-Drying for Natural Dyes:**
    - For naturally dyed fabrics, drying in the sun can help set the dye by gently heating the fibers. Lay the fabric flat in direct sunlight, turning it occasionally to ensure even drying.

Post-Dye Treatments: Ironing and Finishing

After your fabric has been rinsed, unwrapped, and the dye has been set, the final steps are all about giving your project a polished, finished look. Ironing, pressing, and other finishing treatments ensure that the fabric looks clean, crisp, and ready to use in your desired application, whether it's for fashion, home décor, or art.

Ironing the Fabric:

1. **Iron While Damp:**
    - For the smoothest result, iron your fabric while it's still slightly damp. This makes it easier to remove any creases or wrinkles caused by the folding and binding during

the Shibori process. Use a steam iron for best results.
2. **Iron on the Reverse Side:**
    - To preserve the integrity of the dyed patterns, it's best to iron the fabric on the reverse side. This protects the colors from fading due to direct heat and helps avoid any accidental smudging.
3. **Use a Pressing Cloth:**
    - If you need to iron directly on the design side, use a pressing cloth (a thin, clean cloth placed between the iron and your fabric). This prevents the iron from directly touching the fabric and helps maintain the vibrancy of the dye.

Finishing Techniques:

1. **Removing Excess Thread Marks:**
    - If your design has any thread marks or small imperfections from the binding process, now is the time to address them. Gently clip any stray threads or use a seam ripper to carefully remove any unwanted marks without damaging the fabric.
2. **Stretching the Fabric:**

- For fabric projects that need a more tailored finish, stretching the fabric lightly can help it regain its original shape after being bound and dyed. This is especially useful if the fabric will be used in upholstery or framed art pieces.

3. **Final Wash:**
    - After setting the dye and ironing, it's a good idea to give the fabric one final wash in cold water with a gentle detergent to remove any last traces of fixatives or excess dye. This also helps soften the fabric and remove any stiffness from the dyeing process.

Storing Your Finished Fabric:

- **Store in a Cool, Dry Place:** Once your fabric is completely finished, store it in a cool, dry place to preserve its color and condition. Avoid storing it in direct sunlight or humid environments, as these can cause fading or damage to the fabric over time.
- **Hanging or Rolling:** For large pieces of fabric, hanging or rolling them ensures they stay wrinkle-free and prevents any creases that could distort the patterns.

CHAPTER NINE
SHIBORI PROJECTS

Shibori is a versatile art form that transcends its traditional roots, offering a range of applications for both functional and decorative purposes. From home décor to fashion and accessories, the unique patterns and textures achieved through Shibori dyeing can enhance a wide array of items. This chapter explores various Shibori projects, providing detailed guidance and inspiration for incorporating this ancient technique into contemporary creations.

Home Décor: Curtains, Pillows, and Tablecloths

Incorporating Shibori into home décor adds a personalized touch to your living space. The rich patterns and textures of Shibori can transform everyday items like curtains, pillows, and tablecloths into statement pieces that showcase your creativity.

Curtains:

1. **Choosing the Fabric:**
    - Opt for natural fibers like cotton, linen, or silk for curtains, as they absorb dye well and hold patterns effectively. Lightweight

cotton is a popular choice for its drape and ease of use, while linen offers a more textured look.
2. **Preparing the Fabric:**
    - Wash and pre-treat the fabric before dyeing to remove any sizing or finishes that might prevent the dye from adhering evenly. Iron the fabric to remove wrinkles and prepare it for the Shibori techniques you plan to use.
3. **Design Ideas:**
    - **Gradient Effects:** Use dip dyeing techniques to create a gradient effect, transitioning from a deep hue at the top to a lighter shade at the bottom. This adds a serene, ombre effect to your curtains.
    - **Geometric Patterns:** Employ Itajime Shibori to create bold geometric patterns such as diamonds or triangles. The symmetrical designs can add a modern touch to traditional curtain styles.
    - **Organic Designs:** For a more relaxed look, use Kumo or Miura Shibori techniques to create organic, flowing patterns. These designs evoke a sense of natural beauty and movement.
4. **Hanging and Finishing:**

- After dyeing and setting the dye, hang your curtains to check for any imperfections or color inconsistencies. Press them with an iron on the reverse side to ensure a smooth finish. Consider adding lining if you desire additional privacy or light blocking.

Pillows:

1. **Selecting Pillow Covers:**
   - Choose pre-made pillow covers or fabric that suits your pillow form. Cotton or linen is ideal for capturing Shibori patterns effectively. Pre-washing the fabric ensures better dye absorption and prevents shrinkage.
2. **Design Ideas:**
   - **Cluster Patterns:** Create a series of Shibori-dyed pillow covers with matching or complementary patterns. For example, use Kanoko Shibori for one cover and Kumo Shibori for another, creating a coordinated look.
   - **Accent Pillows:** Add a pop of Shibori dye to smaller accent pillows. Experiment with different techniques on small-scale projects to highlight intricate patterns.

3. **Assembly and Finishing:**
    - After dyeing, follow the manufacturer's instructions for sewing or inserting pillow forms. Ensure the fabric is fully dry and ironed before assembling the pillows to prevent any dye transfer or color bleeding.

Tablecloths:

1. **Fabric Selection:**
    - Opt for fabrics that are both durable and dye-friendly, such as cotton or polyester blends. Cotton is particularly good for capturing the details of Shibori patterns.
2. **Design Ideas:**
    - **All-Over Patterns:** Use Shibori techniques like Arashi or Itajime to create all-over patterns for a dynamic tablecloth design. A consistent pattern throughout the tablecloth adds visual interest.
    - **Border Designs:** Create a Shibori border along the edges of a plain tablecloth for a sophisticated touch. This can be achieved by applying techniques like Kumo Shibori to just the edges.
3. **Care and Maintenance:**
    - Ensure that your tablecloth is pre-treated before dyeing and follow care instructions

for washing and maintaining the dye. Regularly clean the tablecloth according to the fabric's requirements to keep the colors vibrant.

Fashion: Scarves, Shawls, and Clothing

Shibori adds a unique touch to fashion items, making scarves, shawls, and clothing stand out with one-of-a-kind patterns and colors. These items are perfect for showcasing the versatility and beauty of Shibori.

Scarves:

1. **Fabric Choices:**
   - Silk and lightweight cotton are popular choices for scarves. These fabrics have a smooth texture and absorb dye well, resulting in vibrant colors and intricate patterns.
2. **Design Ideas:**
   - **Gradient Scarves:** Use dip dyeing to create a gradient effect on scarves, transitioning from one color to another. This technique works well for creating elegant, flowing patterns.

- **Patterned Scarves:** Employ geometric or organic Shibori patterns to create visually striking scarves. Techniques like Kanoko or Miura Shibori can add texture and depth.

3. **Finishing:**
   - After dyeing, carefully wash and iron the scarf. If necessary, hem or finish the edges to prevent fraying and give the scarf a polished look.

Shawls:

1. **Fabric Selection:**
   - Choose fabrics that drape well and have enough surface area to showcase Shibori designs. Wool, silk, and lightweight wool blends are excellent choices for shawls.
2. **Design Ideas:**
   - **Large-Scale Patterns:** Due to the larger surface area, you can experiment with larger Shibori patterns or combinations of techniques. Arashi Shibori can create dramatic diagonal stripes, while Itajime can produce striking geometric shapes.
   - **Ombré Effects:** Apply gradient dyeing to create a subtle, flowing color transition

that enhances the shawl's drape and overall aesthetic.
3. **Assembly and Care:**
    - Finish the shawl by trimming any excess dye or threads and ironing it on the reverse side. For wool shawls, consider using a steamer to avoid damaging the fabric.

Clothing:

1. **Fabric Preparation:**
    - Pre-wash fabric for clothing to ensure it's free of any finishes or sizing. Fabric choices include cotton, linen, and blends that are comfortable and suitable for the intended garment.
2. **Design Ideas:**
    - **Unique Dresses:** Use Shibori techniques like Nui or Arashi to create unique dresses with striking patterns. The dyeing can add an artistic flair to dresses, making them stand out.
    - **Shirts and Tops:** Employ geometric patterns or subtle gradients for shirts and tops. Techniques like Itajime can be used for structured patterns, while Miura

> Shibori offers a more casual, textured look.

3. **Sewing and Finishing:**
   - After dyeing, thoroughly rinse and iron the fabric before cutting and sewing. Follow garment construction steps and ensure that the fabric maintains its integrity through the sewing process.

Accessories: Bags, Hats, and Other Items

Shibori can also enhance a variety of accessories, adding a unique touch to everyday items such as bags and hats. These projects allow for creative experimentation and practical use of Shibori patterns.

Bags:

1. **Fabric Selection:**
   - Choose sturdy fabrics like canvas, denim, or felt that can withstand the rigors of daily use. These fabrics also take dye well and can showcase vibrant Shibori patterns.
2. **Design Ideas:**
   - **Statement Bags:** Use bold Shibori patterns to create eye-catching bags. Techniques like Itajime or Kumo Shibori

can produce distinctive designs that make the bag a standout accessory.
- **Tote Bags:** Employ subtle gradients or organic patterns for tote bags to add a touch of elegance while keeping the design practical.

3. **Assembly and Care:**
   - Ensure the fabric is fully dry and ironed before cutting and sewing the bag. Consider adding a lining for extra durability and to protect the dye patterns.

Hats:

1. **Fabric Choices:**
   - Opt for fabrics like cotton, wool, or synthetic blends that can be shaped into hats and hold dye well. Pre-wash the fabric to ensure even dyeing and prevent shrinkage.

2. **Design Ideas:**
   - **Patterned Brims:** Use Shibori techniques like Kanoko or Miura to create interesting patterns on hat brims. These designs can add a unique touch to classic hat styles.
   - **Gradient Hats:** Apply dip dyeing to create a gradient effect on the entire hat or on

specific sections, such as the crown or band.
3. **Construction and Finishing:**
    - After dyeing and drying, proceed with the hat's construction. Iron and shape the hat as needed, ensuring that the fabric retains its dye patterns and remains in good condition.

Other Items:

1. **Home Accessories:**
    - Items like table runners, placemats, and napkins can also be enhanced with Shibori techniques. Use similar methods as for tablecloths but on a smaller scale.
2. **Personal Accessories:**
    - Explore other personal items like phone cases, wallets, or belts. These small-scale projects offer an opportunity to experiment with Shibori techniques on various materials.

Large-Scale Shibori: Quilts and Wall Hangings

Large-scale Shibori projects, such as quilts and wall hangings, allow for expansive displays of your dyeing skills and creativity. These projects can become centerpiece items in a home or gallery setting, showcasing the intricate beauty of Shibori patterns on a grand scale.

Quilts:

1. **Fabric Selection:**
    - Choose high-quality cotton or cotton blends that are comfortable and hold dye well. Pre-wash all fabric pieces to ensure even dye absorption and to prevent shrinkage after the quilt is assembled.
2. **Design Ideas:**
    - **Panel Quilts:** Use Shibori techniques on individual quilt panels. Each panel can feature a different technique or pattern, creating a cohesive yet varied design.
    - **All-Over Patterns:** Apply techniques like Arashi or Kumo on larger quilt sections for dramatic, continuous patterns.
3. **Assembly and Finishing:**
    - Once the fabric is dyed and dry, cut and piece together your quilt. Follow standard quilting techniques, including layering and stitching. Consider using a gentle fabric setting spray to protect the dye.

Wall Hangings:

1. **Fabric Selection:**
    - For wall hangings, select a fabric that drapes well and is visually appealing, such as silk or linen. These fabrics enhance the overall look of the wall art and hold dye effectively.
2. **Design Ideas:**
    - **Large Panels:** Create large Shibori-dyed fabric panels to be framed or hung as wall art. Use techniques like Itajime or Kanoko to produce striking designs that capture attention.
    - **Tapestries:** Combine various Shibori patterns and colors to make a tapestry that can serve as a focal point in a room. Experiment with layering and mixing techniques for a rich, textured look.
3. **Mounting and Display:**
    - Ensure the fabric is fully dry and ironed before mounting. Use a suitable frame or hanging method that complements the design and allows for proper display.

CHAPTER TEN

TROUBLESHOOTING COMMON SHIBORI PROBLEMS

Even experienced Shibori practitioners can encounter issues during the dyeing process. Troubleshooting common problems effectively can save time and ensure high-quality results. This chapter addresses some frequent issues encountered in Shibori projects and offers solutions to overcome them.

Fixing Uneven Dyeing and Color Bleeding

Uneven dyeing and color bleeding are common issues in Shibori that can affect the overall appearance of your fabric. Addressing these problems requires careful attention to preparation, technique, and post-dyeing care.

Uneven Dyeing:

1. **Causes and Solutions:**
   - **Inconsistent Fabric Pre-Treatment:** Ensure the fabric is thoroughly pre-washed to remove any sizing or finishes that might interfere with dye absorption. Use a consistent

pre-treatment process for even dye uptake.
- **Improper Dye Application:** Uneven dyeing can occur if the dye is not applied uniformly. Ensure the fabric is evenly submerged in the dye bath and agitated gently for uniform coverage.
- **Fabric Folding and Binding Issues:** If the fabric is not folded or bound consistently, it can lead to uneven patterns. Pay careful attention to your folding, binding, or stitching techniques to achieve a more uniform result.

2. **Prevention:**
   - **Test Samples:** Before starting on your main project, test dyeing on small fabric samples to ensure even coverage and correct application methods.
   - **Monitor Dye Concentration:** Ensure the dye concentration is appropriate for the fabric and desired depth of color. Too high or too low concentration can lead to uneven results.

Color Bleeding:

1. **Causes and Solutions:**

- **Inadequate Dye Setting:** Color bleeding often occurs when dye has not been properly set. Use appropriate fixatives according to the dye manufacturer's instructions to prevent bleeding.
- **Incompatible Dyes:** Ensure that the dyes used are compatible with the fabric and with each other. Some dyes may not blend well and can cause bleeding when layered or combined.
2. **Prevention:**
    - **Use Fixatives:** Apply dye fixatives or mordants as recommended to lock in the color and prevent bleeding.
    - **Rinse Thoroughly:** After dyeing, rinse the fabric thoroughly with cold water until the water runs clear to remove excess dye and reduce bleeding.

Addressing Fabric Tearing or Overstretching

Fabric tearing or overstretching can occur during the Shibori process due to the tension applied during binding or the dyeing process itself. Proper handling and technique can mitigate these issues.

Fabric Tearing:

1. **Causes and Solutions:**
    - **Excessive Tension:** Applying too much tension when binding or folding the fabric can lead to tearing. Use moderate tension and avoid overstretching the fabric.
    - **Weak Fabric:** Some fabrics are more prone to tearing due to their construction or quality. Choose high-quality, durable fabrics for Shibori projects and handle them with care.
2. **Prevention:**
    - **Test Fabric:** Test the fabric's strength and flexibility by performing a small sample project before committing to larger pieces.
    - **Gentle Handling:** Handle the fabric gently throughout the process to avoid unnecessary strain and tearing.

Over-Stretching:

1. **Causes and Solutions:**
    - **Improper Binding:** If the fabric is bound too tightly, it can become stretched out of shape. Adjust the tension when binding to ensure a consistent and controlled application.
    - **Dyeing Process:** Prolonged exposure to hot dye baths can cause some fabrics to

stretch. Use dyeing techniques that are appropriate for the fabric type and temperature.
2. **Prevention:**
    - **Correct Binding Techniques:** Use proper binding techniques to avoid excessive stretching. For example, when using rubber bands or threads, ensure they are not too tight.
    - **Follow Fabric Care Instructions:** Adhere to the fabric's care instructions to maintain its original shape and prevent stretching during dyeing.

Avoiding Stains and Unwanted Marks

Stains and unwanted marks can be detrimental to the final appearance of your Shibori project. Proper preparation and handling can help prevent these issues.

Stains:

1. **Causes and Solutions:**
    - **Contaminated Work Area:** Ensure that your workspace is clean and free from contaminants that could transfer to your

fabric. Cover surfaces and use clean tools.
- **Dye Spills:** Handle dye carefully to avoid spills. If spills occur, clean them immediately with water to prevent staining.

2. **Prevention:**
   - **Protect Your Work Area:** Use drop cloths or protective coverings to shield your work area from potential stains.
   - **Wear Protective Gear:** Use gloves and aprons to protect your clothing and skin from dye stains.

Unwanted Marks:

1. **Causes and Solutions:**
   - **Contact with Non-Dyed Areas:** Be cautious of fabric contact with non-dyed areas or other fabrics that might transfer unwanted marks. Use separation layers if necessary.
   - **Improper Drying:** Ensure that the fabric is fully dry before handling it. Wet or damp fabric is more prone to picking up unwanted marks.
2. **Prevention:**

- **Use Clean Tools:** Ensure all tools and materials used in the Shibori process are clean and free from contaminants.
- **Careful Handling:** Handle the fabric carefully to avoid transferring marks from hands or tools.

CHAPTER ELEVEN
THE FUTURE OF SHIBORI

As a timeless art form, Shibori has continuously evolved while maintaining its traditional roots. This chapter explores how Shibori is adapting to the modern world, its impact on contemporary fashion and art, and the artists and designers who are pushing the boundaries of this ancient technique.

How Shibori Continues to Evolve

Shibori, with its rich history and intricate techniques, has found a place in contemporary creativity, bridging the gap between ancient craft and modern aesthetics. The evolution of Shibori reflects its adaptability and the innovative ways it is being reinterpreted in today's world.

Innovation in Techniques:

1. **New Materials and Technologies:**
    - **Synthetic Dyes and Fabrics:** Advances in dye technology have introduced new synthetic dyes that offer a wider range of colors and improved colorfastness. Additionally, synthetic and blended fabrics

are being used alongside traditional fibers, expanding the possibilities of Shibori applications.
- **Digital Printing:** Digital textile printing is being used to replicate Shibori patterns with precision. This technology allows for high-resolution patterns and custom designs that maintain the essence of Shibori while offering new possibilities.

2. **Hybrid Techniques:**
   - **Combining Techniques:** Artists and designers are experimenting with hybrid techniques that blend Shibori with other fabric manipulation methods, such as pleating, smocking, or embroidery. These combinations create unique textures and effects that enhance traditional Shibori patterns.
   - **Integration with Modern Art Forms:** Shibori is being incorporated into contemporary art forms such as installation art and mixed media projects. These integrations showcase Shibori's versatility and its ability to transcend traditional boundaries.

Adaptation in Craftsmanship:

1. **Educational Initiatives:**
   - **Workshops and Online Courses:** With the rise of online learning platforms, Shibori techniques are being taught to a global audience. Workshops and courses offer in-depth training and inspire a new generation of artists and crafters to explore Shibori.
   - **Collaborative Projects:** Collaborations between traditional artisans and modern designers are fostering innovation in Shibori. These partnerships bring fresh perspectives and techniques to the craft, ensuring its continued evolution.
2. **Sustainability Focus:**
   - **Eco-Friendly Practices:** There is a growing emphasis on sustainable practices in Shibori, including the use of natural dyes and eco-friendly fabrics. Artisans are exploring ways to minimize environmental impact while preserving the artistry of Shibori.
   - **Recycled Materials:** Some practitioners are incorporating recycled or upcycled materials into their Shibori projects, reflecting a commitment to both creativity and environmental responsibility.

Shibori in Contemporary Fashion and Art

Shibori's influence extends beyond traditional applications, making significant inroads into contemporary fashion and art. Its distinctive patterns and textures are being reimagined in various creative contexts, influencing trends and inspiring new forms of expression.

Contemporary Fashion:

1. **High Fashion Runways:**
    - **Designer Collections:** Leading fashion designers are incorporating Shibori techniques into their collections, showcasing the art form in haute couture and ready-to-wear garments. Shibori's intricate patterns add depth and sophistication to modern fashion designs.
    - **Textural Innovations:** Designers are experimenting with Shibori's texture and color effects to create garments with unique visual and tactile qualities. The technique's ability to produce rich textures makes it a favored choice for avant-garde fashion pieces.
2. **Streetwear and Casual Fashion:**

- **Custom Apparel:** Shibori has found its way into streetwear and casual fashion, with custom-dyed pieces gaining popularity. Independent designers and DIY enthusiasts use Shibori to create one-of-a-kind garments and accessories that reflect personal style.
- **Sustainable Fashion:** The resurgence of Shibori in sustainable fashion highlights its adaptability to modern trends. By using natural dyes and traditional techniques, designers emphasize eco-conscious fashion choices.

Contemporary Art:

1. **Installation Art:**
    - **Large-Scale Projects:** Shibori patterns and techniques are being used in large-scale installation art, where the fluidity and depth of the technique create immersive environments. These installations often explore themes of texture, color, and form.
    - **Interactive Art:** Some artists are incorporating Shibori into interactive art pieces, where viewers can engage with the patterns and textures in innovative

ways. These works often invite participants to experience the art form firsthand.
2. **Mixed Media:**
    - **Textile Art:** Shibori is increasingly featured in mixed media art, where it is combined with other materials such as paper, metal, and found objects. This approach adds new dimensions to Shibori's traditional applications and expands its artistic potential.
    - **Collaborations:** Collaborations between textile artists and other art forms, such as painting and sculpture, are resulting in unique artworks that highlight Shibori's versatility and contemporary relevance.

Artists and Designers Inspired by Shibori

A new wave of artists and designers is drawing inspiration from Shibori, infusing the traditional technique with contemporary creativity. These individuals and groups are pushing the boundaries of Shibori, exploring its potential in innovative and unexpected ways.

Influential Artists:

1. **Traditional and Contemporary Artists:**
    - **Artists Combining Shibori with Modern Techniques:** Contemporary artists who blend Shibori with digital and mixed media techniques are expanding the craft's boundaries. Their works often feature Shibori patterns in new contexts, challenging traditional perceptions.
    - **Global Artists:** Shibori's influence extends beyond Japan, with artists worldwide adopting and adapting the technique. International exhibitions and collaborations highlight the global reach and impact of Shibori.
2. **Emerging Talents:**
    - **Young Creatives:** Emerging artists and designers are experimenting with Shibori in innovative ways, often incorporating it into fashion, home décor, and visual art. Their fresh perspectives and experimental approaches are shaping the future of Shibori.

Leading Designers:

1. **Fashion Designers:**
    - **High-Profile Collections:** Renowned fashion designers are incorporating

Shibori into their collections, elevating the technique to high fashion levels. These designers often reinterpret traditional patterns to fit contemporary aesthetics.
- **Innovative Applications:** Designers are exploring new ways to apply Shibori, including unconventional fabric treatments and novel design concepts. Their work pushes the envelope of Shibori's potential in fashion.

2. **Textile and Home Décor Designers:**
   - **Functional Art:** Textile and home décor designers are using Shibori to create functional yet artistic pieces, such as upholstery, curtains, and rugs. These designs often emphasize the technique's textural and visual qualities.
   - **Collaborative Projects:** Collaborative projects between Shibori artisans and home décor designers result in unique products that blend traditional craft with modern design principles.

CHAPTER TWELVE

CONCLUSION

Shibori, with its rich history and intricate techniques, offers a transformative journey for anyone willing to explore its depths. As you delve into the world of Shibori, you uncover not just a craft but a dynamic art form that bridges tradition and innovation. This conclusion aims to guide you in finding your unique Shibori style, encourage creativity, and reflect on the art's profound impact.

Finding Your Unique Shibori Style

One of the most exciting aspects of Shibori is its ability to be personalized and adapted to fit your individual artistic vision. As you experiment with various techniques and patterns, you'll discover what resonates with your style and preferences.

Exploring Different Techniques:

1. **Experimentation:**
    - **Try Multiple Techniques:** Don't hesitate to explore and combine various Shibori techniques, from traditional methods like Kanoko and Arashi to modern

adaptations. Each technique offers unique possibilities and can contribute to your signature style.
- **Create Samples:** Develop sample swatches using different techniques and dyes to see how they work together. This experimentation will help you understand the nuances of each method and how they can be applied to your projects.

2. **Developing a Signature Look:**
   - **Find Your Aesthetic:** Identify the patterns and color combinations that you are drawn to. Whether you prefer bold geometric designs or delicate, organic patterns, let these preferences guide your creations.
   - **Incorporate Personal Elements:** Add personal touches to your Shibori projects, such as using fabrics and colors that reflect your style or cultural background. This will make your work truly unique.

Mastering Technique and Style:

1. **Continuous Learning:**
   - **Attend Workshops:** Participate in workshops or online courses to learn new techniques and refine your skills.

Continuous learning will help you stay inspired and improve your craft.
- **Seek Feedback:** Share your work with fellow artists or online communities to receive constructive feedback. This can provide valuable insights and help you grow as a Shibori artist.

2. **Create a Portfolio:**
   - **Document Your Work:** Keep a portfolio of your Shibori projects, including photographs and descriptions of your techniques and inspirations. This will not only help you track your progress but also showcase your unique style.

Encouraging Creativity and Experimentation

Shibori is a canvas for creativity and experimentation. Embracing this aspect of the art form can lead to innovative and exciting results. Here are some ways to foster creativity in your Shibori practice:

Push the Boundaries:

1. **Innovative Approaches:**
   - **Mix Techniques:** Combine traditional Shibori techniques with contemporary methods to create new effects. For

example, layer different patterns or experiment with unusual dyeing techniques.
- **Explore New Mediums:** Apply Shibori techniques to unconventional materials or objects. This could include home décor items, mixed media art, or even installation pieces.

2. **Experiment with Colors and Patterns:**
   - **Unconventional Color Palettes:** Experiment with unusual color combinations and gradients. The ability to create striking and unexpected color effects can lead to unique designs.
   - **Pattern Variations:** Play with variations of traditional patterns or develop your own. This experimentation can lead to fresh and innovative patterns that set your work apart.

Foster a Creative Environment:

1. **Create a Studio Space:**
   - **Dedicated Workspace:** Set up a dedicated space for your Shibori projects where you can experiment freely and comfortably. A well-organized workspace

can enhance your creativity and productivity.
- **Inspirational Surroundings:** Surround yourself with inspirational materials, such as fabric swatches, color samples, and examples of Shibori art. This can stimulate creativity and keep you motivated.

2. **Collaborate and Share:**
    - **Join a Community:** Engage with Shibori communities or art groups to share ideas, techniques, and inspiration. Collaboration can spark new ideas and provide support.
    - **Teach and Learn:** Consider teaching others about Shibori or participating in collaborative projects. Sharing your knowledge and learning from others can deepen your understanding and appreciation of the craft.

Final Thoughts on the Art of Shibori

Shibori is more than just a method of dyeing fabric; it is an art form that encompasses history, technique, and personal expression. Its beauty lies in the intricate patterns and textures that result from a harmonious blend of traditional craftsmanship and modern innovation.

Reflecting on the Journey:

1. **Appreciate the Craft:**
   - **Embrace Tradition and Innovation:** Recognize the historical significance of Shibori while embracing the opportunities for innovation and modern interpretation. This balance will enrich your practice and keep the craft relevant.
   - **Celebrate Achievements:** Take pride in your Shibori creations and the skills you have developed. Celebrate your accomplishments and use them as motivation to continue exploring and growing as an artist.
2. **Look Forward:**
   - **Future Possibilities:** Consider the future of Shibori and how you can contribute to its evolution. Stay open to new ideas, techniques, and collaborations that will shape the craft's ongoing journey.
   - **Pass on the Art:** Share your passion for Shibori with others, whether through teaching, creating, or exhibiting your work. By passing on the knowledge and enthusiasm for Shibori, you help ensure its continued vitality and growth.

Shibori offers a magical world of creativity and expression. By finding your unique style, encouraging experimentation, and reflecting on the art's impact, you can fully embrace the richness and beauty of Shibori. Whether you are a seasoned practitioner or a new enthusiast, the art of Shibori invites you to explore its endless possibilities and make your mark in its evolving legacy.

Made in the USA
Las Vegas, NV
28 February 2025